ear Parent:
ur child's love of reading starts here!

ry child learns to read in a different way and at his or her own
ed. Some go back and forth between reading levels and read
rite books again and again. Others read through each level in
er. You can help your young reader improve and become more
fident by encouraging his or her own interests and abilities. From
ks your child reads with you to the first books he or she reads
he, there are I Can Read Books for every stage of reading:

SHARED READING
Basic language, word repetition, and whimsical illustrations,
ideal for sharing with your emergent reader

BEGINNING READING
Short sentences, familiar words, and simple concepts
for children eager to read on their own

READING WITH HELP
Engaging stories, longer sentences, and language play
for developing readers

READING ALONE
Complex plots, challenging vocabulary, and high-interest topics
for the independent reader

ADVANCED READING
Short paragraphs, chapters, and exciting themes
for the perfect bridge to chapter books

an Read Books have introduced children to the joy of reading
e 1957. Featuring award-winning authors and illustrators and a
lous cast of beloved characters, I Can Read Books set the
dard for beginning readers.

fetime of discovery begins with the magical words **"I Can Read!"**

*Visit www.icanread.com for information
on enriching your child's reading experience.*

For Treeske . . . you have
the most fun! —R.S.

I Can Read Book® is a trademark of HarperCollins Publishers.

Splat the Cat: Up in the Air at the Fair
Copyright © 2014 by Rob Scotton
www.icanread.com

Library of Congress catalog card number: 2013951080
ISBN 978-0-06-211596-6 (trade bdg.) —ISBN 978-0-06-211595-9 (pbk.)

13 14 15 16 17   LP/WOR   10 9 8 7 6 5 4 3 2 1   ❖   First Edition

Splat the Cat

Up in the Air at the Fair

Based on the bestselling books by Rob Scotton

Cover art by Rick Farley

Text by Amy Hsu Lin

Interior illustrations by Robert Eberz

HARPER

An Imprint of HarperCollins*Publishers*

It was finally the day of the fair!
Splat, Spike, and Plank knocked
on Kitten's door.

While the friends waited for Kitten,

they did stretches.

They wanted to prepare

for every ride and game at the fair.

At last Kitten came out . . .

in a wheelchair!

"What happened?" asked Splat.

"I fell down the stairs,"

said Kitten.

"I can't go to the fair."

Everyone signed Kitten's cast.
Then Splat, Spike, and Plank
waved good-bye,
and off to the fair they went.

"Poor Kitten," Plank said.

"I wish we could share the fun of the fai

"We can," said Splat.

"Let's bring Kitten something

back from the fair!"

MOUSE

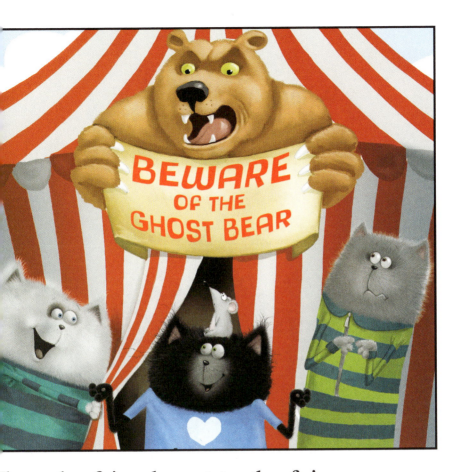

hen the friends got to the fair,

e first tent they saw had a spooky sign:

WARE OF THE GHOST BEAR.

ѕo in if you dare!" said Spike.

Ѵo way," said Plank. "Too creepy."

 don't care," Splat said.

When Splat came out
of the ghost bear's lair,
he had spiky hair.

"I wasn't really scared,"
Splat declared.
"What's next?"

Then the friends heard a cry.

"Shop in here! Lots to wear!"

"How about a fun hat for Kitten?"

asked Spike.

"It might mess up her hair,"

said Splat.

Another voice blared,

"Are you hungry? Try my wares!"

Plank picked up a chocolate éclair.

"Yum!" he said.

"Kitten would love these!"

The friends went on the next ride.

And Spike took care

of the chocolate éclairs.

When they got off,

Plank and Splat stared at Spike.

He had cream all over his face.

No more éclairs for Kitten!

"Sorry, I was hungry," said Spike.

"We'll get more," said Splat.

"For Kitten, we've got money to spare

They went back to the food booth.

"Now what?" said Plank in despair.

"Let's ride the Ferris wheel,"
Splat said. "I think better
when I'm up in the air."

The friends went up, and up, and up.

Plank said, "Wow! What a view!"

Spike said, "It's so unfair

that Kitten couldn't be here, too."

Splat spotted a game from the air.

We can win a stuffed teddy bear

for Kitten!" said Splat.

The cat in charge of the booth
explained the game.
Splat would get a pair
of coconuts to throw.

If Splat hit the square,

the cat in the chair

would fall into the water tank.

Splat would win a prize.

"Okay," said Splat. "Here I go!"

He threw the first coconut.

The coconut fell on Spike's foot.

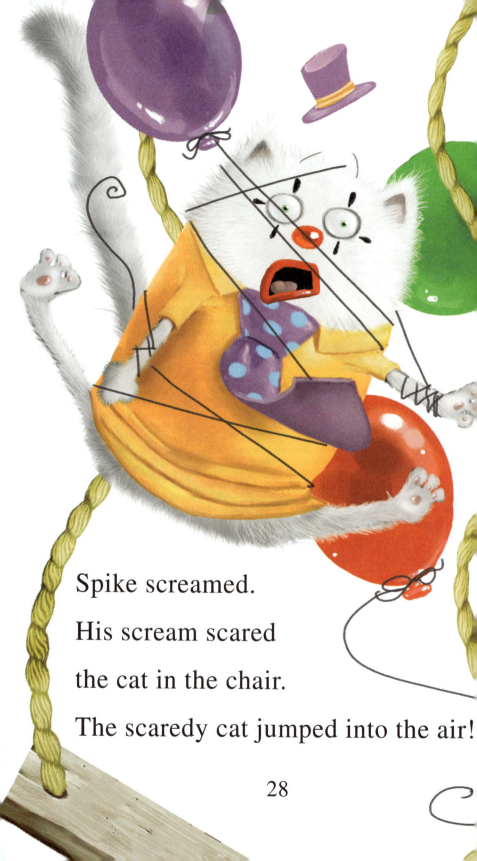

Spike screamed.

His scream scared

the cat in the chair.

The scaredy cat jumped into the air!

"Look what you've done!"

said the booth owner.

He gave Splat a glare.

It was time to leave the fair!

The friends helped the scaredy cat

get untangled from the balloons.

The grateful cat gave Splat, Spike,

and Plank the balloons.

The friends took the balloons home

to give to Kitten.

"It's nice to know how much you care,"
said Kitten.

"I'm lucky to have friends
with flair."